LEWIS AND CLARK TRAIL

THE PHOTO JOURNAL

IN MEMORY OF MY DAD, GEORGE W. THOMAS

BORN FEBRUARY 22, 1916

BUTTE, MONTANA

His spirit will live forever in the hearts of all who knew him.

LEWIS AND CLARK TRAIL

THE PHOTO JOURNAL

Up the Missouri, down the Columbia and back

BY GEORGE THOMAS

SNOWY MOUNTAIN PUBLISHING

P.O. Box 667, Harlowton, Montana 59036.

(406) 632-4602, EMAIL ggthomas@mcn.net

CONTENTS

FOREWORD

This collection of photographs is called, "Lewis and Clark Trail—The Photo Journal" for good reason. The attention to detail and accuracy earns the title "*The* Photo Journal." If Lewis and Clark had had the good fortune to document their amazing journey with photographs, these are the scenes that would have been recorded because they are the scenes described in their journals. Each photograph was taken within three weeks of the date Lewis and Clark camped at or passed each location—thus, landscapes, water flows and vegetative stages are very much as seen by expedition members. The entire route is carefully followed from Camp Dubois on the Mississippi River to Fort Clatsop on the Pacific Ocean and *back*.

The author's text is presented solely to guide the reader along the trail. The perspective is from that of European man and does not attempt to capture the Native American perspective.

You may detect a fence post, a ranch road or other trappings of modern civilization; however, the scenes are very much as beautiful and dramatic as they were two hundred years ago. Quotes from the original journals were carefully selected to capture the feelings and emotions of the men as they forged their way through each day's landscapes. The original spelling and grammar were retained to better capture the unique color and flavor of the authors. All journal quotes are from Capt. Lewis, Capt. Clark, Sgt. Gass, Sgt. Ordway and Pvt. Whitehouse and are from, *The Journals of the Lewis and Clark Expedition*, editor Gary Moulton—University of Nebraska Press. Place names are those used in the journals—modern names appear in parentheses.

INTRODUCTION

In 1800 the vast unknown lands west of the Mississippi River were claimed by some, controlled by no one and sought after by all. French and British influence over the fur trade dominated the Missouri River as far as the Mandan Indian villages, some 1,600 miles from St. Louis. Spain had claimed everything west of the Mississippi River. Russia had designs on the coastal west as well. In 1801 Spain ceded all of the Louisiana Territory back to France, although Spain continued to control it politically.

The United States had a destiny to own the West when American Capt. Robert Gray discovered the mouth of the "Great Western River" in 1792 and named it Columbia, after his ship. For years, Thomas Jefferson had visualized the United States spanning from the Atlantic to the Pacific. He had an obsession for these unexplored lands beyond the Mississippi. He had a powerful curiosity for the Indian tribes, the potential for trade and commerce, and the possibility for a water route to the Pacific.

When Jefferson was elected President in 1801 he already had plans to explore the western frontier, although the Louisiana Purchase wouldn't take place for another two years. A sense of urgency spurred him since the British had already sent Alexander MacKenzie across Canada to the Pacific Ocean. MacKenzie had found some rivers out west, but none were navigable enough for trade routes. The door was still open for discovery and control of the Columbia River and its vast trade potential. Jefferson hired Army Captain Meriwether Lewis as his private secretary for the purpose of preparing to lead such an expedition. Capt. Gray had already established the longitude and latitude of the mouth of the Columbia River. All that was needed now was to explore a route from the Missouri River to the mouth of the Columbia.

Jefferson and Lewis spent the next year strategizing the trip. The team of Jefferson and Lewis was perfect—Jefferson had the power and influence to guide Lewis to the best experts on botany, geography, astronomy, mineralogy and ethnology. Lewis had the best library of books and maps of the continent at his disposal. He obtained medical training from one of the leading physicians of the time. Learning how to preserve and label biological specimens was a high priority.

In 1802 Jefferson asked permission from Spain to explore the Missouri River system and was denied. Defying the denial, he sent a secret message to Congress in January of 1803 asking for an appropriation of $2,500 to cover the costs of an expedition. Congress readily approved the requested appropriation, the expedition's goals were set, and Lewis began purchasing supplies. The latest rifles and ammunition topped the list. Next in priority was enough paper and ink to archive daily events and discoveries. The list of equipment was influenced by the myths that there was either a water passage to the Pacific Ocean or that any portage would be quick and easy, that the climate was moderate, the ground fertile and the river navigable year-round, not freezing over in the winter.

President Jefferson gave instructions to Lewis on the importance of mapping the Missouri River and exploring that river to its furthest extension. Jefferson's inquisitive mind was coming up with endless questions to answer about the lives of the western natives—their language, their living conditions, with whom they traded and how far they roamed.

A major goal was that the commercial potential of the western country be examined and recorded. Persuading the Indians to accept and trust the Americans as their new trading partner would be a major challenge for Lewis. Jefferson made it clear to Lewis that he should avoid conflict with the natives. Some of the tribes, such as the Teton Sioux, were powerful and sometimes cantankerous. The size of the expedition was debated. Too many could cause the Indians to be alarmed. Too few would leave the party easy prey for an aggressive tribe. The complexities of planning soon made it clear that another officer was needed. It took Lewis little time to select William Clark—a man with whom he had served in the Army some years before. Clark was knowledgeable of the ways of the wilderness, and dealing with Indians was his specialty. He was not as formally educated as Lewis, but his solid temperament and ability to deal with problems under pressure more than made up for his lack of education. Lewis and Clark were very different. Time would prove this difference to be an advantage for their success. Both men were very confident, but Lewis was moody and had a temper while Clark was more relaxed and had an uncanny ability to solve problems among his men and with the Indians, as well.

Lewis arranged for a boat to be built in Pittsburgh. The craft was a flat-bottom, 55-foot keel boat which was designed to be rowed, sailed, pushed, poled or pulled. The keel boat had eleven oar locks on each side, a stout mast and was able to haul a ten-ton load.

Gifts for the natives were critical to their acceptance of the strangers. Trinkets consisted of beads, ribbons, cloth, mirrors and flags. More substantial presents included a specially-minted peace and friendship coin, knives, awls, fishhooks and tomahawks.

An experimental, collapsible metal-frame boat was designed to be used when the river became too shallow for the bigger boats. The frame could be reassembled on the spot and covered with animal hides. In theory it would be light to carry and could haul large loads, requiring very little water in which to navigate.

The summer of 1803 found Lewis purchasing and arranging for supplies to be sent west to Pittsburgh by wagon train. The keel boat construction was behind schedule due to the drinking habits of the boat builder. Lewis spent many agonizing weeks waiting for his keel boat to be finished so supplies could be boated down the Ohio River. During this time he picked up a new traveling companion—a big, black Newfoundland.

Finally, on August 30, 1803, Lewis and a crew of eleven made their way down the Ohio River to Clarksville, Indiana Territory, where Clark, his slave, York, and a few selected soldiers were waiting. Lewis and Clark had Presidential authority to select whomever they wanted as members of their party from the military posts along their route to the Mississippi River. The keel boat with its crew of potential explorers made its way down the Ohio to the Mississippi. Once on the "Big" river they rowed their way up river just past St. Louis to the mouth of Wood River, located on the east shore of the Mississippi across from the mouth of the Missouri. Here at Camp Dubois they spent the winter, training and making the final selection of men for the upcoming adventure.

Lewis spent much of the winter just down river in St. Louis. He was not only gathering more supplies, but he was also gleaning as much information as he could from the fur trappers who had plied the Missouri River.

Spring was in the air. The anxiety of the young explorers was as high as the river water.

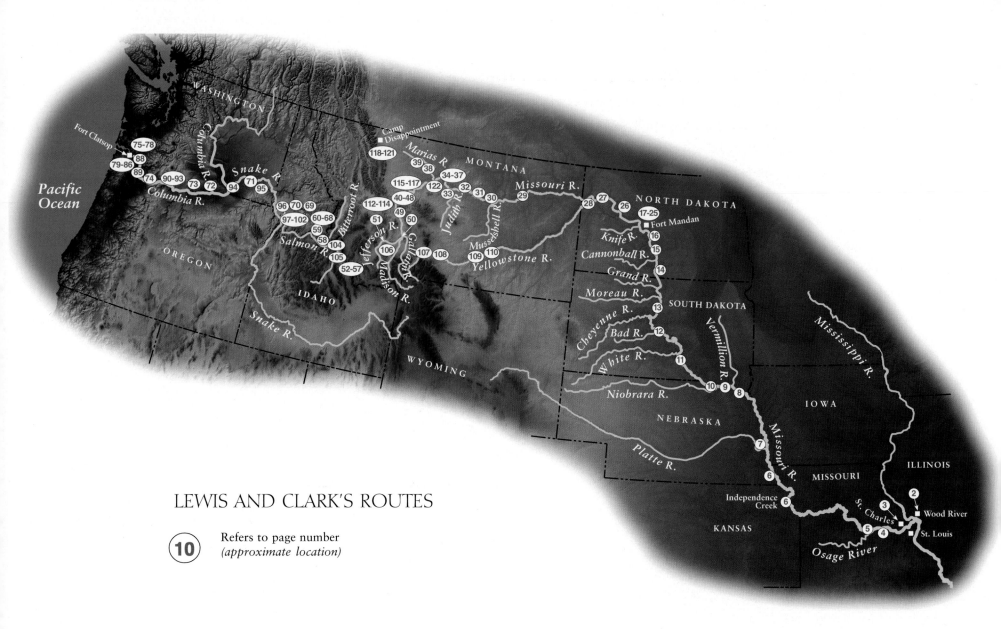

Pacific
Ocean

Fort Clatsop

WASHINGTON

Camp
Disappointment

MONTANA

Marias R.

NORTH DAKOTA

Fort Mandan

Knife R.

Cannonball R.

Grand R.

Moreau R.

SOUTH DAKOTA

Cheyenne R.

Bad R.

White R.

Vermillion R.

IOWA

Mississippi R.

Columbia R.

Snake R.

Missouri R.

Bitterroot R.

Judith R.

Musselshell R.

Yellowstone R.

OREGON

Salmon R.

Jefferson R.

Madison R.

Gallatin R.

IDAHO

Snake R.

Columbia R.

WYOMING

Niobrara R.

NEBRASKA

Platte R.

MISSOURI

ILLINOIS

St. Charles

Wood River

St. Louis

Independence
Creek

KANSAS

Osage River

LEWIS AND CLARK'S ROUTES

10   Refers to page number
(approximate location)

PART ONE

CAMP DUBOIS TO THE MANDAN VILLAGES

WOOD RIVER MOUTH AT THE MISSISSIPPI RIVER, CAMP DUBOIS   DECEMBER 12, 1803 TO MAY 14, 1804

Lewis and Clark's Corps of Discovery nosed out from the Wood River, crossed the Mississippi and started up the Missouri which was rushing bank full from the snow melt. The adventure had begun for the forty men and a dog.

Set out from … Dubois at 4 oClock P.M. and … proceeded on under a jentle brease

—CLARK, MAY 14, 1804

at 2 o'clock in the afternoon arrived at St. Charles … This is an old French village; in the country around which, a number of Americans have settled. We remained at St. Charles until the 21st, where Captain Lewis arrived from St. Louis and joined us.

—Gass, May 16, 1804

MISSOURI RIVER AT ST. CHARLES   MAY 16 TO 21, 1804

Lewis had been in St. Louis finishing up some last minute business. The crew spent one day rearranging supplies on the keel boat, which had been overloaded in the stern causing the bow to ride up on logs instead of pushing them aside.

On May 21st the complete Corps of Discovery is on the Missouri, struggling to move the heavily laden keel boat along with two smaller flat bottom boats called "pirogues." Capt. Clark, being the more experienced boatman, was usually in charge of the boats. Capt. Lewis spent most of his days walking along the banks and hills, searching for new plants and animals to collect. Also on shore were the hunters on horseback usually led by George Drouillard, a Canadian and Shawnee.

TAVERN CAVE, 30 MILES UP RIVER FROM ST. CHARLES   MAY 23, 1804

MISSOURI RIVER NEAR ST. JOHN   MAY 25, 1804

on S Side land handsome the Soil Rich—high Banks, encamped at a French village ... called St. John, this is the last Settlement of whites on this River.
—ORDWAY, MAY 25, 1804

halted at an endented part of a Rock which juted over the water, Called by the french the tavern which is a Cave
—CLARK, MAY 23, 1804

RIVER BLUFFS ON THE NORTH BANK
MAY 28, 1804

Lewis came close to death when he slipped and nearly fell off the limestone cliff while exploring the cave and bluffs.

15 MILES DOWN RIVER FROM OSAGE
RIVER, SPRING FLOODING
(AUXVASSE CREEK)   MAY 30, 1804

OSAGE RIVER, JUST ABOVE MOUTH TO MISSOURI RIVER   JUNE 1, 1804

Fur traders returning down river from the wilderness were always questioned about river conditions and Indian tribes that lay ahead. The Corps of Discovery was anxious to meet some of the Indians of the region, but this time of year most of the tribes were out on the plains hunting buffalo.

Discipline problems such as sleeping while on watch or sneaking whiskey in these early days of the journey were dealt with by whippings—the standard military remedy.

above the mouth of Osage River
Larb Side, Camped ... a fair
after noon
                    —CLARK, JUNE 1, 1804

INDEPENDENCE CREEK MOUTH ENTERING THE MISSOURI   JULY 4, 1804

this day is the 4th of July,
we name this Independance
us. Creek
— CLARK, JULY 4, 1804

The crew fired the keel boat cannon and brought out an extra ration of whiskey for the July 4th celebration.

MISSOURI RIVER CAMPSITE   JULY 14, 1804

Lewis notes how forceful the Platte was where it enters the Missouri. Getting past this shallow spot proved to be a pushing and pulling ordeal because of the sand and mud.

The sediment it deposits, consists of very fine particles of white sand while that of the Missoury is composed principally of a dark rich loam.

—LEWIS, JULY 21, 1804

PLATTE RIVER, IN FOREGROUND, FLOWING INTO THE MISSOURI RIVER
JULY 21, 1804

COUNCIL BLUFF, COVERED WITH TREES
SITE OF COUNCIL AND CAMP
JULY 30 TO AUGUST 4, 1804

The first encounter with Indians was a disappointment at this place they named "Council Bluff." The Oto and Missouri Indians were not interested in making peace with their long-standing enemies—the Pawnee and Omaha; however, they were impressed with the keel boat's cannon blast.

below the High Bluff we came to in a grove of timber and formed a Camp ... this Prarie is Covered with grass

—CLARK, JULY 30, 1804

hief Blackbird of the Omaha nation and four hundred tribal
members had died from smallpox four years earlier and were
buried on this hill.

A few days later, Sgt. Floyd died from what Lewis called,
"Biliose Chorlick." Most likely it was from a ruptured appendix.
He would be the only member of the Corps of Discovery to die on
the entire expedition.

CHIEF BLACKBIRD HILL   AUGUST 11, 1804

*we landed at the foot of the hill on
which Black Bird ... was buried ... from
the top of this hill may be Seen the
bends or meanderings of the river*
—CLARK, AUGUST 11, 1804

WHITE STONE RIVER
(VERMILLION RIVER)
AUGUST 24-25, 1804

SPIRIT MOUND   AUGUST 25, 1804

ewis and Clark and nine men hiked from the White
Stone River (Vermillion River) to investigate the
mound. The local Indians believed it was the residence of
18-inch high devils with very sharp arrows that, at a great
distance, could kill anyone who approached.

*from the mouth of White Stone river ... in an imence Plain
a high Hill is Situated, and appears of a Conic form*
—CLARK, AUGUST 24, 1804

CALUMET BLUFFS   AUGUST 29 TO SEPTEMBER 1, 1804

The Yankton Sioux encountered here were not impressed with the trivial gifts that Lewis and Clark had passed out. They were more interested in obtaining guns and ammunition. The Sioux were anxious to begin trading with the Americans but Lewis had to inform them that this was not a trade mission but rather a diplomatic venture to set the stage for the future.

proceded on—pass Calumet Bluff of a yellowish read & a brownish white Hard clay
    —CLARK, SEPTEMBER 1, 1804

MISSOURI RIVER, QUICOURRE RIVER
(NIOBRARA RIVER) MOUTH AT FAR LEFT
SEPTEMBER 4, 1804

*Came to at the mouth of Qui courre this river ... Spreds over a
large Surface ... it has a Great many Small Islands & Sand bars*

—CLARK, SEPTEMBER 4, 1804

George Shannon, the youngest of the explorers, became lost while hunting. Many days later the half-starved Shannon was found and this river was named in his honor.

SHANNON RIVER   SEPTEMBER 14, 1804

HIGH WATER CREEK (ANTELOPE CREEK)   SEPTEMBER 23, 1804

TETON RIVER (BAD RIVER) NEAR MOUTH   SEPTEMBER 24-28, 1804

MISSOURI RIVER CAMPSITE, 8 MILES BELOW TETON RIVER (BAD RIVER)
SEPTEMBER 23, 1804

Three boys from the Teton Sioux Tribe swam from High Water Creek (Antelope Creek) across the Missouri to inform the expedition that there were large Indian camps at the Teton River (Bad River). The prairies had already been set ablaze to warn the camps of the approaching white men. Lewis and Clark sent word with the boys that they wanted to call a council the next day.

The Teton Sioux had a reputation for being the largest, most powerful, most ruthless and most feared on the Missouri River. The expedition's first meeting with the Teton Sioux was nearly disastrous. Clark's boat was held for ransom when he and his men attempted to leave after unproductive gift giving and council. Clark drew his sword and prepared for battle. Chief Black Buffalo finally interceded and allowed them to leave.

SIOUX SYMBOLS

Just below these hills Lewis and Clark met Jean Valle, a French trapper and trader, at his small cabin. He had spent the previous year up the Cheyenne River near the Black Hills.

I walked up this River a mile,
Saw the tracks of white bear, verry large
    —CLARK, OCTOBER 7, 1804

On the banks of this river Clark found the first grizzly bear tracks.

As the expedition moved farther up river they discovered that the tribes were less nomadic and lived in earthen lodges. The Arikara, Hidatsa, and Mandan cultivated corn and squash. This area was a major trade center for the plains Indians as well as for white men who had connections to the British and French fur trading companies.

MOREAU RIVER, A MILE UP FROM THE MOUTH AT THE MISSOURI   OCTOBER 7, 1804

The Arikara were amazed by York, Clark's slave. The natives had never seen a black man and York played to his audience by making himself appear to be half wild. Clark's October 10th quote concerning York: "he Carried on the joke and made himself more turribal than we wish him to doe."

Lewis and Clark had a difficult time accepting the warfare between the various tribes. Skirmishes with the neighboring tribes were a way of life.

ARIKARA COUNCIL SITE, ON THE WEST BANK OF THE MISSOURI
OCTOBER 10 TO 12, 1804

WEST BANK TRIBUTARY TO THE MISSOURI   OCTOBER 13, 1804

CANNONBALL RIVER, FLOCK OF PELICANS   OCTOBER 18, 1804

MISSOURI RIVER AT THE ABANDONED (DOUBLE DITCH VILLAGE)   OCTOBER 22, 1804

passed a Small Island at the head of which is a bad place, an old Village ... the Mandans occupied about 25 years ago
—CLARK, OCTOBER 22, 1804

The "bad place" refers to the abandoned village which had been decimated by a smallpox epidemic.

THE ABANDONED (DOUBLE DITCH VILLAGE)
OCTOBER 22, 1804

Saw great nos. of Buffalow

—CLARK, OCTOBER 20, 1804

Great Deel of Beaver Sign

—CLARK, OCTOBER 22, 1804

MISSOURI RIVER   OCTOBER 25, 1804

passed a verry bad riffle
of rocks
    —CLARK, OCTOBER 25, 1804

MISSOURI RIVER CAMPSITE, JUST BELOW
MANDAN/HIDATSA VILLAGES   OCTOBER 26,1804

KNIFE RIVER, HIDATSA VILLAGE SITE   OCTOBER 27, 1804

RECONSTRUCTED HIDATSA EARTH LODGE,
BUFFALO SKULLS ON ROOF FOR "GOOD MEDICINE"

*the houses are round and
Verry large Containing
Several families*
    —CLARK, OCTOBER 27, 1804

The boat was made from buffalo hide stretched over bent limbs, fur side out to keep it watertight. Lewis and Clark noted that these Mandan/Hidatsa boats were very seaworthy.

RECONSTRUCTED MANDAN/HIDATSA LODGE INTERIOR

"BULL BOAT"

It was time to "hole up" for the winter—the river was icing, the Mandan/Hidatsa were friendly and had food for trade. The Corps of Discovery had now traveled some 1600 miles and were at the edge of their maps. This was the limit of all previously known white man's western progress. From here on it was truly the vast unknown.

A modest fort was quickly erected where there were plenty of cottonwood trees. The winter was bitter. Clark refined his extensive maps of the Missouri River, its tributaries, landscape, and inhabitants. Lewis recorded the life and ceremonies of the neighboring natives, and worked on his wildlife and plant collections. Hunting, visiting and trading kept the men occupied. Staying warm and fed was a challenge during the short, frigid days.

In November of 1804 Toussaint Charbonneau and one of his wives, Sacagawea, were hired as interpreters for the trip beyond. Sacagawea was a Shoshone who had been captured by a Hidatsa raiding party near the headwaters of the Missouri. The Hidatsa had sold her to Charbonneau. She was only sixteen years old and pregnant.

FORT MANDAN SITE   NOVEMBER 2, 1804

This morning early we fixed on the site for our fortification which we immediately set about.
—LEWIS, NOVEMBER 2, 1804

Fort Mandan was located some seven miles down river from the mouth of the Knife River.

FORT MANDAN REPLICA

NEAR THE SITE OF FORT MANDAN   FALL 1804

SANDSTONE FORMATION NEAR THE SITE OF FORT MANDAN   FALL 1804

NEAR FORT MANDAN SITE   WINTER 1804–05

blew verry hard ... Snow Drifting from one bottom to another
                    —CLARK, DECEMBER 28, 1804

WINTER HUNTING GROUNDS NEAR FORT MANDAN   WINTER 1804–05

MISSOURI RIVER, FROZEN SILENCE   WINTER 1804–05

*Soome Snow to day; 8 men
go to hunt the buffalow*
    —CLARK, JANUARY 3, 1805

MANDAN/HIDATSA EARTH LODGE REPLICA

FORT MANDAN REPLICA

PART TWO

FORT MANDAN TO THE PACIFIC

The ice on the river was beginning to break up by the end of March. The big keel boat, piloted by Corp. Warfington and a small crew, was loaded with all the specimens, journals and maps and launched down river to St. Louis.

The Corps of Discovery began paddling up the river April 7, 1805, in six dugout canoes and the two pirogues. There were now thirty-three members including Sacagawea and her two-month old baby boy, Jean Baptiste.

Capt. Lewis headed north along the east bank on foot. After a long winter at the fort with endless hours of desk work he needed the exercise, plus it gave him time to contemplate the long trip ahead.

MISSOURI RIVER, BETWEEN FORT MANDAN AND THE MANDAN/HIDATSA VILLAGES   APRIL 7, 1805

we were now about to penetrate a country ... on which the foot of civillized man had never trodden

—LEWIS, APRIL 7, 1805

we proceeded on our Voyage, and passed the 2nd Mandan Village, and a River lying on the South side of the Mesouri
—WHITEHOUSE, APRIL 8, 1805

KNIFE RIVER   APRIL 8, 1805

proceed on to oure encampment, which was ... opposite to a high bluff
—LEWIS, APRIL 8, 1805

MISSOURI RIVER, HIGH BLUFF ON SOUTHWEST BANK   APRIL 8, 1805

PASQUE FLOWER

I saw flowers in the
praries to day
      —CLARK, APRIL 9, 1805

Ice on the river has broken up, but melts slowly on the Missouri in early spring.

the Bluffs ... formed
of a mixture of
yellow clay and
sand—many
horizontal stratas of
carbonated wood
      —LEWIS, APRIL 9, 1805

MISSOURI RIVER BLUFFS   APRIL 9, 1805

BRANT ON MISSOURI RIVER   APRIL 13, 1805

a Gange of brant pass

      —CLARK, APRIL 13, 1805

MISSOURI RIVER, SOUTHWEST BANK   APRIL 18, 1805

WEST SIDE OF THE MISSOURI   APRIL 16, 1805

The boatmen often battled fierce headwinds, which greatly impeded progress.

I ascended the hills from whence I had a most pleasing view of the country, perticularly of the wide and fertile vallies formed by the missouri and the yellowstone rivers
—LEWIS, APRIL 25, 1805

YELLOWSTONE RIVER, A FEW MILES UP FROM THE MISSOURI   APRIL 25, 1805

T he prairie was just turning green, and animal life was every-where. Hunting for the meat supply was now an easy task with an abundance of buffalo, elk, deer and antelope. The men celebrated their arrival at the confluence of the two great rivers with extra whiskey, fiddle music, and "hilarity dancing & singing."

the river Jaune is shallow, and the Missouri deep and rapid …We encamped on the point
—GASS, APRIL 26, 1805

CONFLUENCE OF THE MISSOURI AND YELLOWSTONE RIVERS
A FRENCH TRANSLATION FOR THE YELLOWSTONE WAS RIVER ROCHEJAUNE
APRIL 26, 1805

MISSOURI RIVER   MAY 3, 1805

passed large bottoms of timber, &
plains on each Side but no high hills
— ORDWAY, MAY 3, 1805

The plains Indians had warned the party about grizzly bears. At first the men were anxious to "take on" the great bear, but soon discovered their guns were inadequate and had many close calls with wounded bears.

On clear nights Lewis would determine their position with his astronomical sightings. He calculated they were now 2,000 miles into their journey.

MISSOURI RIVER CAMPSITE   MAY 19, 1805

MISSOURI RIVER, ONE MILE UP RIVER FROM SACAGAWEA CREEK   MAY 21, 1805

MISSOURI RIVER AND (LITTLE ROCKY MOUNTAINS)   MAY 21, 1805

the shores are abbrupt and bould
and composed of a black and
yellow clay
                    —LEWIS, MAY 21, 1805

The days are getting warmer. Distant mountains stir the adrenaline.

Some of the party yesterday discovered
a high range of mountains to the west
                    —WHITEHOUSE, MAY 21, 1805

MISSOURI RIVER CAMPSITE   MAY 25, 1805

WOOD ROSE

the Country on each Side is high
broken and rocky ... the air of this
country is pure & healthy.
                    —ORDWAY, MAY 25, 1805

Missouri River   May 28, 1805

JUDITH RIVER   MAY 29, 1805

Clark named this river in honor of Julia, "Judith," Hancock of Virginia, whom he was planning to court upon his return.

MISSOURI RIVER   MAY 31, 1805

we proceeded on our Voyage, and passed high white Clifts of rocks, and some high pinnacles which was 100 feet high
—WHITEHOUSE, MAY 31, 1805

each wall retains the same thickness at top which it possesses at bottom.
—LEWIS, MAY 31, 1805

MISSOURI RIVER   MAY 31, 1805

MISSOURI RIVER CAMPSITE   MAY 31, 1805

The Hills and river Clifts of this day exhibit a most romantick appearance

—CLARK, MAY 31, 1805

MISSOURI RIVER JUNE 1, 1805

(HIGHWOOD MOUNTAINS) JUNE 2, 1805

we Saw a high mountain to
the west of us
  —WHITEHOUSE, JUNE 2, 1805

The Mandan and Hidatsa had not mentioned this fork in the river. Lewis and Clark surmised that the south fork must come from the Rocky Mountains because it was clearer than the muddy north fork. Most of the men figured the north fork must be the true Missouri because it looked more like the muddy Missouri that they were used to seeing. The correct choice was critical because the Corps of Discovery was under orders from President Jefferson to follow the Missouri to its source and then on to the Pacific Ocean.

Lewis took six men to explore the north river, while Clark and five men went up the south river. While Lewis and Clark explored, the remainder of the men stashed the large red pirogue and buried much of the heavier baggage and supplies. The load had to be lightened with the river becoming shallow and the supplies would be needed on the return trip.

MARIA'S RIVER (MARIAS RIVER) CAMPSITE AT MISSOURI RIVER CONFLUENCE
LEWIS NAMED THE RIVER IN HONOR OF HIS COUSIN, MARIA WOOD
JUNE 3–11, 1805

which of these rivers was the Missouri
—LEWIS, JUNE 3, 1805

MARIA'S RIVER (MARIAS RIVER) CAMPSITE OF LEWIS PARTY   JUNE 5, 1805

Clark was convinced by the second day out that he was on the Missouri and returned to base camp. Lewis ventured almost 40 miles before he felt for sure that this northern stream was too far north and would be the wrong choice.

encamped ... in a handsome well timbered bottom

—LEWIS, JUNE 5, 1805

MARIA'S RIVER (MARIAS RIVER)   JUNE 5, 1805

Capt. Lewis and Pvt. Goodrich were the first documented white men to see the Great Falls of the Missouri. Not only was it a glorious sight, but more importantly it confirmed they were on the right river. The next day Lewis had more surprises—four more falls blocked their way to navigable waters.

THE GREAT FALLS OF THE MISSOURI   JUNE 13, 1805

I hurryed down the hill ... to gaze on this sublimely grand specticle.
—LEWIS, JUNE 13, 1805

The Great Falls of the Missouri   June 13, 1805

(Rainbow Falls)   June 14, 1805

PORTAGE CAMPSITE, JUST BELOW PORTAGE CREEK
(BELT CREEK)   JUNE 16 TO 28, 1805

MISSOURI RIVER RAPIDS AND CAMPSITE   JUNE 15, 1805

*Came to a bad rapid which we
concluded to not undertake ... so
we Camped*
　　　—WHITEHOUSE, JUNE 15, 1805

*Part of the men were employed in taking the canoes up
the small river about a mile and an half; and some
engaged in making small waggons to haul the canoes
and loading above the falls. Captain Clarke and 4 men
went to view and survey our road to the place where
we were to embark above the falls. Opposite the mouth
of the small river, a beautiful sulphur spring rises out of
the bank ...*
　　　—GASS, JUNE 17, 1805

Near the portage campsite they dug a cache and buried more supplies and the white pirogue.

Sacagawea became extremely ill here. Lewis administered a mixture of bark and opium and washed it all down with water from the sulphur spring. She quickly recovered.

SULPHUR SPRINGS   JUNE 17, 1805

SULPHUR SPRINGS FALLS   JUNE 17, 1805

It took many trips and three weeks to portage the canoes and supplies over the 18-mile route.

PORTAGE CREEK (BELT CREEK)   JUNE 17, 1805

INCLINE WHERE THEY PULLED THE CANOES AND SUPPLIES
OUT OF PORTAGE CREEK (BELT CREEK)   JUNE 17, 1805

ABOVE PORTAGE CAMPSITE ON THE MISSOURI   JUNE 25, 1805

river inclosed between high Steep hills Cut to
pieces by revines but little timber

       —CLARK, JUNE 25, 1805

Lewis supervised the metal frame boat building at the upper river portage camp. The boat was dubbed "the experiment." The metal strap framework was hauled all the way from Virginia to be assembled and covered with 28 elk hides and 4 bison skins. The labor-intensive project proved to be a major disappointment when the boat leaked badly and was soon abandoned. Clark quickly selected trees and had a crew hollow out two dugout canoes to replace the failed "experiment."

On July 15th, eight cottonwood dugout canoes were loaded and back on navigable waters. There was now a sense of urgency. They needed to find Sacagawea's Shoshone Tribe to acquire horses to pack their supplies over the mountains. It was mid-July, the days were getting shorter, and they hadn't seen an Indian since they left the Mandans.

the prickly pear is now in full blume and forms one of the beauties as well as the greatest pests of the plains.
—LEWIS, JULY 15, 1805

at this place there is a large rock ... it is insulated from the neighbouring mountains
—LEWIS, JULY 16, 1805

MISSOURI RIVER   JULY 16, 1805

MISSOURI RIVER   JULY 18, 1805

GATES OF THE ROCKY MOUNTAINS   JULY 19, 1805

this curious looking place we call the gates of the Rocky Mountains
—ORDWAY, JULY 19, 1805

arived at the 3 forks of the Missourie

        —Whitehouse, July 27, 1805

Three Forks of the Missouri   July 27, 1805

Sacagawea recognized the three forks as the place where a Hidatsa war party had attacked her band of Shoshone and kidnapped her five years earlier.

Lewis and Clark named the south fork Gallatin's River after Albert Gallatin, Secretary of Treasury, the middle fork Madison's River after James Madison, Secretary of State, and the southwest fork Jefferson's River after President Thomas Jefferson.

Another decision had to be made at these three forks in the river. Jefferson's River was the most logical choice as it seemed to flow from the mountains they needed to cross.

walked up the S.E. fork about ½ a mile and
ascended the point of a high limestone clift

        —Lewis, July 27, 1805

Gallatin's River, a half mile up from the mouth   July 27, 1805

JEFFERSON'S RIVER (JEFFERSON RIVER)   AUGUST 3, 1805

we have to double man the canoes and drag them over the
Sholes and rapid places.

—ORDWAY, AUGUST 3, 1805

BEAVER'S HEAD (BEAVERHEAD ROCK)   AUGUST 8, 1805

the Indian woman recognized the point of
a high plain ... this hill she says her
nation calls the beaver's head
        —LEWIS, AUGUST 8, 1805

S acagawea informed Lewis and Clark that this area was the
  summer retreat for her people. The pass over the mountains
to her Shoshone Nation was just ahead.

JEFFERSON'S RIVER (NOW NAMED THE BEAVERHEAD RIVER AT THIS POINT)
AUGUST 10, 1805

(Horse Prairie)   August 11, 1805

he suddonly turned his hose about, gave him the whip
leaped the creek and disapeared in the willow brush

—Lewis, August 11, 1805

Lewis had gone ahead on foot with Shields, McNeal, and Drouillard in search of the Shoshone Tribe. While they explored they surprised an Indian on horseback. The young brave was curious but he fled when Lewis attempted to gain his trust.

The expedition was at the end of its navigable waters. They had wrangled the canoes up Jefferson's River as far as they could.

LICHEN ENCRUSTED ROCK
ALONG THE TRAIL

LEWIS AND HIS MEN CONTINUED UP THE INDIAN TRAIL TO THE WEST   AUGUST 12, 1805

the road took us to the most distant
fountain of the waters of the mighty
Missouri in surch of which we have spent
so many toilsome days
                    —LEWIS, AUGUST 12, 1805

(TRAIL CREEK)   AUGUST 12, 1805

(Continental Divide-Lemhi Pass) east side   August 12, 1805

(CONTINENTAL DIVIDE-LEMHI PASS) WEST SIDE   AUGUST 12, 1805

For the first time they were leaving United States' territory and entering the Columbia River system.

we proceeded on to the top of the dividing ridge from which I discovered immence ranges of high mountains still to the West

—LEWIS, AUGUST 12, 1805

*I now decended the mountain about ¾ of a mile ...
here I first tasted the water of the great Columbia river*
—LEWIS, AUGUST 12, 1805

(AGENCY CREEK) ¾ MILE WEST OF (LEMHI PASS)   AUGUST 12, 1805

Lewis realized that the hope of finding an easy overland route to the Columbia River and on to the Pacific Ocean was vanishing. They soon found the Shoshone Tribe and Chief Cameahwait. Lewis traded supplies for horses and persuaded the Shoshone to help pack their gear over the divide. Meanwhile, back on Jefferson's River, Clark and his crew were still working their way toward the mouth of (Horse Prairie Creek).

Lewis and his men now had horses and a band of Indians willing to help. On August 15th, they headed back over the pass to rendezvous with Clark at Camp Fortunate (so named because they were fortunate to get horses).

Sacagawea could finally be used as a translator. The translation chain was tenuous. Sacagawea would speak Shoshone with the Indians and translate it into Hidatsa. Then Charbonneau would translate Hidatsa into French to Private Labiche, who would then translate French to English. Sacagawea recognized Chief Cameahwait as her brother soon after the complex communications began. This happy reunion cemented the critical relationship with the Shoshone.

(LEMHI CREEK) WHERE THE SHOSHONE VILLAGE WAS LOCATED AUGUST 13–15, 1805

The elusive route to the Columbia was much discussed. Finally, an old Shoshone, named "Old Toby" by Lewis and Clark, agreed to guide them over the only route he knew. Clark, not wanting to give up on a more direct water route, explored Lewis' River (Salmon River) even though the Indians had informed him that the river was not navigable. After several days of hiking, Clark realized the Indians were right. The waters were much too swift and shallow for canoes, and the banks were too steep and rocky for horse travel. It is no wonder this river is called "The River of No Return."

On August 30th the Corps of Discovery regrouped, bid farewell to the Shoshone, and headed north with their new guide, "Old Toby."

LEWIS' RIVER (SALMON RIVER)   AUGUST 24, 1805

The river at this place is so confined ...
and very rapid
—GASS, AUGUST 24, 1805

(LOST TRAIL PASS)   SEPTEMBER 3, 1805

RED BELT FUNGUS

went up and down the mountains all day.
   —WHITEHOUSE, SEPTEMBER 3, 1805

Some of the fir trees ... are covred with warts
   —ORDWAY, SEPTEMBER 3, 1805

The explorers encountered the Salish near here and managed
to trade for a few more horses.

(Bitterroot Range, Trapper Peak)   September 6, 1805

The valley is become more extensive, and our creek has increased to a considerable river.
—Gass, September 7, 1805

Clark's River (Bitterroot River)   September 7, 1805

TRAVELLERS REST CREEK (LOLO CREEK) FLOWING
INTO CLARK'S RIVER (BITTERROOT RIVER)
SEPTEMBER 9, 1805

*encamped on a large creek which falls in on
the West as our guide informes that we should
leave the river at this place*

—LEWIS, SEPTEMBER 9, 1805

Old Toby also warned them that game would be scarce
as they headed west.

TRAVELLERS REST CREEK (LOLO CREEK) CAMPSITE   SEPTEMBER 9–11, 1805

*great size the rocks on the Side of
the Mountain*
      —CLARK, SEPTEMBER 13, 1805

(LOLO HOT SPRINGS)   SEPTEMBER 13, 1805

ROCKS ON THE HILL NEXT TO THE HOT SPRINGS
SEPTEMBER 13, 1805

*I found this water nearly boiling hot at the
places it Spouted from the rocks*
      —CLARK, SEPTEMBER 13, 1805

*We passed over a dividing ridge
... we encamped ... up which
there are some prairies*
          —GASS, SEPTEMBER 13, 1805

(PACKERS MEADOW) CAMPSITE   SEPTEMBER 13, 1805

(LOLO PASS)   SEPTEMBER 14, 1805

Looking west, they realized there were still more mountains to traverse.

FLATHEAD RIVER (LOCHSA RIVER)   SEPTEMBER 14, 1805

Rations were running low, and there was no game to be found. Old Toby was trying to follow the old Nez Perce trail but ended up on a fishing path down to the river. They headed back up the steep ridge to find the main trail after they discovered their mistake.

the river ... Swift and Stoney, here we wer compelled to kill a Colt for our men & Selves to eat

—CLARK, SEPTEMBER 14, 1805

(Whitehouse Pond)   September 15, 1805

Steep assents & to pass the emence
quantity of falling timber
        —Clark, September 15, 1805

Lewis and Clark trail (Wendover Ridge)
September 15, 1805

(Wendover Creek) September 15, 1805

we crossed a creek
a Small pond
        —Whitehouse,
        September 15, 1805

The Corps of Discovery stopped to water the horses in preparation for the climb back to the ridge in search of the Nez Perce trail.

NEZ PERCE TRAIL   SEPTEMBER 16, 1805

We were all surprized when we awoke this morning; to find ourselves covered with snow
—WHITEHOUSE, SEPTEMBER 16, 1805

The shortage of food was becoming critical. They had to forge their way through these mountains before they starved. They trudged through heavy wet snow as they climbed over one mountain ridge after another for the next three days. Captain Clark led a small party in search of food, but they could only find a stray horse and a couple grouse.

SINQUE HOLE CAMPSITE
SEPTEMBER 17, 1805

camped at a ... Sinque hole full of water
—WHITEHOUSE, SEPTEMBER 17, 1805

(Bitterroot Mountains)   September 20, 1805

encamped in a small open bottom where
there was tolerable food for our horses.
—Lewis, September 21, 1805

Collins Creek (Lolo Creek) campsite
September 21, 1805

The Corps of Discovery had survived their mountain ordeal. Finally, the half-starved explorers were out of the snow. At a Nez Perce village they gorged on plentiful salmon and camas root and promptly became violently ill.

the pleasure I now felt having tryumphed over
the rocky Mountains
—Lewis, September 22, 1805

KOOS KOOS KEE RIVER (CLEARWATER RIVER)   SEPTEMBER 26, 1805

Lewis and Clark came down from Weippe Prairie and crossed the river at this location.

Chief Twisted Hair of the Nez Perce was a great help as he assisted in the setting up of camp and hollowing out of pine trees for dugout canoes for the run down to the Columbia River.

a clear pleasant morning ... crossed the River at a shole place the water to the horses belleys. we proceeded on down the South Side and formed an Encampment
—ORDWAY, SEPTEMBER 26, 1805

Koos Koos Kee rapids (Clearwater River)
October 7, 1805

Koos Koos Kee reflections (Clearwater River)   October 8, 1805

proceded on passed 10 rapids
which wer danjerous
    —Clark, October 7, 1805

The party stayed at canoe camp from September 26 to October 6 building canoes. Provisions for the return trip were stashed before launching the canoes. The horses were left in Twisted Hair's care.

The Salmon River (at this point the Snake River) had been named Lewis' River near Lemhi Pass.

The rapids and rocks were challenging. Usually they would shoot the rapids but sometimes portages were required.

MOUTH OF DREWYER'S RIVER (PALOUSE RIVER)
NAMED FOR GEORGE DROUILLARD   OCTOBER 13, 1805

LEWIS' RIVER (SNAKE RIVER)   OCTOBER 12, 1805

MOUNT HOOD   OCTOBER 29, 1805

the top is covered with Snow
—CLARK, OCTOBER 29, 1805

COLUMBIA RIVER   OCTOBER 29, 1805

Saw 4 Cascades caused by Small Streams
falling from the mountains

—CLARK, OCTOBER 30, 1805

JUST BELOW THE CASCADES,
NEAR THE COLUMBIA RIVER
OCTOBER 30, 1805

(MULTNOMAH FALLS)   OCTOBER 30, 1805

Chinook Indians came to the camp by boat and traded fish, wappato roots, and dog—all relished by the wet and weary men.

See great numbers of water fowls ... a high mountn. to the S.W. about 20 miles
—CLARK, NOVEMBER 7, 1805

COLUMBIA RIVER   NOVEMBER 7, 1805

SHALLOW BAY (GRAYS BAY)   NOVEMBER 7, 1805

Great joy in camp we are in View of the Ocian
— CLARK, NOVEMBER 7, 1805

In reality, there was more estuary to cross before actually seeing the Pacific Ocean.

NORTH SHORE COLUMBIA RIVER   NOVEMBER 9, 1805

SHALLOW BAY (GRAYS BAY)   NOVEMBER 9, 1805

*Drift trees which is verry thick
on the Shores*
        —CLARK, NOVEMBER 9, 1805

got a Safe place ... and formed a Campment ... at the enterence of a
Small drean which we found verry convt. on account of its water.

—CLARK, NOVEMBER 10, 1805

POINT DISTRESS (POINT ELLICE) CAMPSITE
NOVEMBER 10–15, 1805

Constant rain kept the explorers pinned down at their dismal camp. Besides a few ducks, hunting was poor. Fortunately, the local Chinooks would come by with salmon and roots for trade.

South from Cape Disappointment, toward the mouth of the Columbia
(so named because they found no trading vessel when they reached the ocean)
November 18, 1805

*the water appears verry shole from off the
mouth of the river from a great distance*
—Clark, November 18, 1805

NORTH FROM CAPE DISAPPOINTMENT   NOVEMBER 18, 1805

men appear much Satisfied with their trip
beholding with estonishment the high waves
dashing against the rocks & this emence ocian
                    —CLARK, NOVEMBER 18, 1805

THE COVE JUST NORTH OF CAPE DISAPPOINTMENT   NOVEMBER 18, 1805

CHINOOK RIVER AT HALEYS BAY (BAKER BAY)   NOVEMBER 19, 1805

The Chinook village at this site had a population of nearly four hundred and was comprised of twenty-eight wood plank houses.

Chennook River Crossed in the Canoe
—CLARK, NOVEMBER 19, 1805

The Corps of Discovery had pushed as far west as possible. Now it was time to find a place to spend the winter.

The Clatsop Indians from the southern shore of the Columbia told them about a herd of elk on the south side of the river. A meat supply was very important, along with shelter and clean water. They considered going back up the river where it would be drier, but their trading goods and other supplies were extremely low and staying near the mouth of the Columbia would increase their chance of spotting a trade vessel.

A vote was taken to determine where they would spend the winter. It was unheard of for minorities or women to vote, but Sacagawea and York (the black slave) voted just like everyone else. They voted to head south across the Columbia where the elk were. Lewis and a small party located a site for their winter quarters a short distance up the Netul River (Lewis and Clark River).

The Corps of Discovery arrived at this location on December 7, 1805. The fort was constructed next to a clear spring.

FORT CLATSOP'S WATER SOURCE

NETUL RIVER (LEWIS AND CLARK RIVER), SITE OF FORT CLATSOP
(NAMED AFTER THE CLATSOP INDIANS—THEIR CLOSEST NEIGHBORS)
DECEMBER 7, 1805

at the Sea Cost near those
Indins I found ... a kind of Bay
... with a high pt. about 4 miles
below.

— CLARK, DECEMBER 10, 1805

NORTH OF (TILLAMOOK HEAD)   DECEMBER 10, 1805

SALT-MAKING KILN LOCATION (TILLAMOOK HEAD)
DECEMBER 10, 1805

Salt was desperately needed to preserve meat. Clark and a few men explored the ocean beach searching for a place for making salt. The point Clark referred to was what he called "Point Clark view" (Tillamook Head or Clarks Point of View).

The right sized rocks were found for a kiln that would support five boiling kettles. Sea water was then boiled down to a fine white sea salt.

Winter at their dismal fort was very depressing. There were only twelve days without rain.

The Chinook and Clatsop Indians were difficult to bargain with, but at least they were peaceful.

Lewis and Clark had plenty of time and took great care to describe the coastal Indians' culture, tools, weapons, and their impressive carved canoes.

rainy & wet ... we all moved in
to our new Fort, which our
officers name Fort Clatsop
—ORDWAY, DECEMBER 25, 1805

FORT CLATSOP REPLICA WINTER 1805–06

Indians informed Lewis and Clark of a beached whale located south of the salt kilns near a large rock (Haystack Rock). Clark took a group of men and Sacagawea to the whale and traded for 300 pounds of blubber and oil to supplement their diet.

(HAYSTACK ROCK)   JANUARY 8, 1806

TIDAL POOL AT (HAYSTACK ROCK)
JANUARY 8, 1806

inoumerable rocks of emence Sise out at a great distance from the Shore
—CLARK, JANUARY 8, 1806

PART THREE

FORT CLATSOP TO TRAVELLERS REST

NETUL RIVER (LEWIS AND CLARK RIVER)   MARCH 23, 1806

The expedition loaded their canoes and bid farewell to Chief Comowool of the Clatsop. He was rewarded for his friendship by giving him Fort Clatsop.

at 1 P.M. we bid a final adieu to Fort Clatsop.
—Lewis, March 23, 1806

passed another point of land
called point William by our
officers ...We encamped at that
place having come 16 Miles
—WHITEHOUSE, MARCH 23, 1806

Point William (Tongue Point) campsite   March 23, 1806

On the Columbia they found that spring runoff had raised the water level, causing the current to be stronger than what they had experienced the previous fall.

COLUMBIA RIVER CAMPSITE   MARCH 31 TO APRIL 6, 1806

Our officers agreed to stay at this place,
until our hunters kill 9 or 10 Elk & Jerk the
meat to take with us.
—WHITEHOUSE, APRIL 2, 1806

BEACON ROCK   APRIL 6, 1806

*this remarkable rock which stands on the North
shore of the river is unconnected with the hills*
—LEWIS, APRIL 6, 1806

COLUMBIA RIVER GORGE   APRIL 10, 1806

The Columbia River became very difficult to navigate. They were forced to portage some of the rapids. To make matters worse, the Indians were becoming more difficult to deal with.

these are the greates theives and scoundrels we have met with.
—LEWIS, APRIL 11, 1806

MOUNT HOOD   APRIL 12, 1806

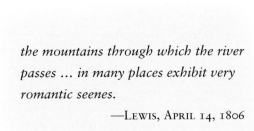

the mountains through which the river passes … in many places exhibit very romantic seenes.

—LEWIS, APRIL 14, 1806

COLUMBIA RIVER   APRIL 14, 1806

While the crew struggled with the canoes and thievery of the Indians, the decision was made to find some horses and abandon canoe travel. Clark went on ahead to trade elk skins, clothes, buttons and even medical practice for pack horses.

By April 20th they finally had enough horses to leave the river. Lewis had become so angry with the Indians that he ordered all spare poles, paddles, and a canoe be burned and said he would shoot the next Indian who attempted to steal from them.

*we continued our march along a narrow rocky
bottom on the N. side of the river*
      —LEWIS, APRIL 23, 1806

COLUMBIA RIVER, NORTH BANK APRIL 23, 1806

COLUMBIA RIVER, FROM THE MOUTH OF THE WALLA WALLA RIVER   APRIL 28, 1806

The day was fair, and we got all our baggage transported to the south side of the river. Here are a great many of the natives encamped on a large creek …We encamped on the creek

—GASS, APRIL 29, 1806

WALLA WALLA RIVER CAMPSITE   APRIL 29, 1806

Chief Yelleppit of the Walla Walla tribe welcomed Lewis and Clark back to his village. They had had a brief but pleasant meeting with him the previous October. The next three days were spent visiting, trading, dancing and singing with the Walla Wallas and the Yakimas. Yelleppit gave Clark a fine white horse. Clark in turn gave the Chief his sword plus some ammunition. Lewis considered the Walla Wallas to be the most honest and sincere people they had met on their voyage.

(Touchet River)   May 2, 1806

*steered East ... over a hilly road along
the N. side of the Creek*

—Lewis, May 2, 1806

*we ascended hills ... thence
down this creek ... to it's
entrance into Lewis's river*

—Lewis, May 4, 1806

The party had arrived back in Nez Perce country. The Indians helped identify the best routes.

Lewis' River (Snake River) at mouth of (Alpowa Creek)   May 4, 1806

Mosquito Creek (Big Canyon Creek)   May 7, 1806

down a steep and lengthey hill
to a creek which we called
Musquetoe Creek
                    —Lewis, May 7, 1806

Lewis and Clark located Twisted Hair, the Chief responsible for keeping the horses over the past winter. It took a few days to round them up but they found most of the herd. The next day Lewis sent a few men down to collect the saddles and ammunition they had stashed the year before.

the road led us up a steep and high hill
                    —Lewis, May 8, 1806

Hills above the Koos Koos Kee River (Clearwater River)   May 8, 1806

Koos Koos Kee River (Clearwater River)   May 13, 1806

proceeded down ... to the river ... Here we halted to wait for a canoe
—Gass, May 13, 1806

The spring runoff had the river running high and fast. The local Nez Perce helped them move their supplies to the other side with canoes.

CAMPSITE MAY 14 TO JUNE 10, 1806

A heavy snowpack in the mountains dictated that the expedition wait nearly a month before continuing on. They set up their camp at the ruins of an ancient Indian fortification. It was a sunken circle about 4 feet deep with a 30 foot diameter. They placed all their gear in the center and put up the tents around the perimeter of the circle.

we formed our Camp around this celler ...
celler had formerly been a wintering house
—ORDWAY, MAY 15, 1806

The Nez Perce were friendly and the area proved to have plentiful game. On June 10th the party packed up and moved to higher ground, just to be closer to the mountains.

Lewis and Clark made final preparation for the assault on the mountains. The Indians warned them of deep snow lingering in the high country. The explorers' spirits were running high, so on June 15th they set out.

we Camped here for a fiew days to kill some deer ... Smooth prarie ... covred with cammass which is now all in blossom
—ORDWAY, JUNE 10, 1806

NEAR WEIPPE PRAIRIE CAMPSITE   JUNE 10 TO 15, 1806

(SMALL PRAIRIE) CAMPSITE   JUNE 15, 1806

Camped at a Small glade
where was pleanty of feed
for our horses
—ORDWAY, JUNE 15, 1806

JUNE 17, 1806

This was the first time that the Corps of Discovery was forced to retreat. They returned to lower country so the horses could graze and waited a week before trying it again.

This time they hired the Nez Perce to guide them over the mountains to Travellers Rest Creek (Lolo Creek). They left on June 24th and made it through to Travellers Rest in just six days.

we found ourselves invelloped in snow
from 8 to 12 feet deep ... we therefore
Come to the resolution to return
—CLARK, JUNE 17, 1806

(Bitterroot Mountains) on the (Nez Perce Trail)   June 27, 1806

from this place we had an extencive view
of these Stupendous Mountains

—Clark, June 27, 1806

This campsite at the hot springs was a welcome treat for the sore and tired travelers. A day later they were back at their Travellers Rest campsite of the last September. They spent the next several days resting and strategizing their return routes.

Clark and his group were to proceed back over the Continental Divide to Camp Fortunate on Jefferson's River. Ordway and ten men were to take the stashed canoes down the Jefferson's and Missouri Rivers to the Great Falls where they were to join Lewis' portage crew.

Clark was to take a few men and all the horses down Jefferson's River to the Three Forks where he was to head overland to explore the Yellowstone, build canoes and float down to the Missouri to meet Lewis' party. Sgt. Pryor and two men planned to drive the horses to the Mandan village.

Lewis with nine men on horses were to continue to follow the Nez Perce trail up the Cokahlahishkit River (Blackfoot River), over the Continental Divide, and down to the Great Falls of the Missouri. At the Great Falls, six of the men were to dig up the cache, portage the falls, and float the Missouri to Maria's River and wait. Lewis was to go north from the Great Falls with three men to explore Maria's River and its tributaries, then meet the rest of his men back at the mouth of Maria's River.

TRAVELLERS REST CREEK (LOLO CREEK)   JUNE 29, 1806

arived at the hot Stream where we
Camped … a number of the party as
well as myself bathed in these hot
Springs … makes the Skin Smart
—ORDWAY, JUNE 29, 1806

PART FOUR

CLARK'S RETURN TRIP

On July 3rd, Clark headed up Clark's River (Bitterroot River). Just before getting to the pass they had crossed the previous fall, they found the Indian trail that headed east over the Continental Divide. This trail was a shorter route to the canoes on the Jefferson's but it would bypass the Shoshone villages. Sacagawea was instrumental in guiding Clark back to the canoes and eventually to the Yellowstone River.

WESTSIDE CONTINENTAL DIVIDE (GIBBONS PASS)
JULY 6, 1806

CAMP CREEK CAMPSITE   JULY 5, 1806

we Camped on the branch & plain
        —ORDWAY, JULY 5, 1806

a fair morning ... proceed on as usal up the branch to the mount.
        —ORDWAY, JULY 6, 1806

(BIG HOLE VALLEY AND MOUNTAINS)   JULY 6, 1806

beheld an open boutifull Leavel Vally ... around
which I could see high points of Mountains
                                                    —CLARK, JULY 6, 1806

At Camp Fortunate they found the cache and canoes in good shape. The men spent the next few days making paddles and preparing for the float down the river.

The river current was running with them and the river was becoming larger as they floated downstream.

JEFFERSON'S RIVER (JEFFERSON RIVER)   JULY 11, 1806

ON THE OVERLAND TRAIL TO CAMP FORTUNATE
(BALDY MOUNTAIN, IN BACKGROUND)   JULY 8, 1806

EASTSIDE (BOZEMAN PASS)   JULY 15, 1806

The indian woman has been of great Service
to me as a pilot through this Country

     —CLARK, JULY 13, 1806

Clark and his men left the larger group
and headed overland.

Yellowstone River and (Crazy Mountains)   July 15, 1806

there is a high rugid Mtn ... bearing North 15 or 20 miles.

—Clark, July 15, 1806

POMPY'S TOWER (POMPEYS PILLAR)   JULY 25, 1806

*arived at a remarkable rock ... This
rock I shall Call Pompy's Tower ...
I marked my name and the day of
the month & year*
—CLARK, JULY 25, 1806

Clark was not able to find adequate trees for dugout canoes so he continued on with the pack train until the 19th of July when they constructed two canoes, strapped them together and headed down the Yellowstone.

Sgt. Pryor, who was driving the horses, only made it a short distance before Crow Indians stole the horses. Pryor then constructed two Mandan-style bull boats made from buffalo hides and eventually caught up to Clark.

Clark named this rock after Sacagawea's son, "Little Pomp."

Yellowstone River, at Pompy's Tower (Pompeys Pillar)   July 25, 1806

on the Northerly Side of the river high romantic Clifts approach

—Clark, July 25, 1806

PART FIVE

LEWIS' RETURN TRIP

COKAHLAHISHKIT RIVER (BLACKFOOT RIVER)   JULY 4, 1806

Lewis' party followed Clark's River (Bitteroot River) down, then traveled up the Cokahlahishkit Valley (Blackfoot Valley), over the Continental Divide and on to the Great Falls of the Missouri.

I now continue my rout up the N. side of the Cokahlahishkit river through a timbered country
—LEWIS, JULY 4, 1806

up through a handsome
narrow plain
      —LEWIS, JULY 7, 1806

(ALICE CREEK DRAINAGE)   JULY 7, 1806

POND NEAR (BROWNS LAKE)   JULY 6, 1806

passed a large crooked pond.
      —LEWIS, JULY 6, 1806

*this gap which is low and an easy
ascent on the W. side*

           —LEWIS, JULY 7, 1806

WEST SIDE OF THE CONTINENTAL DIVIDE (LEWIS AND CLARK PASS)   JULY 7, 1806

EAST SIDE OF THE CONTINENTAL DIVIDE (LEWIS AND CLARK PASS)   JULY 7, 1806

*we came to the dividing ridge
between the waters of the
Missouri and Columbia*

           —GASS, JULY 7, 1806

TORRANT RIVER (DEARBORN RIVER)   JULY 8, 1806

passed torrant river ... this stream comes from the S.W. out of the mountains
                                    —LEWIS, JULY 8, 1806

SHISHIQUAW MOUNTAIN (HAYSTACK BUTTE)   JULY 8, 1806

the Shishiquaw mountain is a high insulated conic mountain

—LEWIS, JULY 8, 1806

MEDICINE RIVER (SUN RIVER) CAMPSITE   JULY 9, 1806

through a handsome level wide bottom
                —LEWIS, JULY 9, 1806

Opening the cache near the Great Falls was a disappointment for Lewis. Spring flood waters had destroyed most of his biological specimens.

Lewis, Drouillard, and the Field brothers headed north to explore Maria's River on the 16th of July.

the rok ... lies in horizontal stratas and makes
it's appearance in the bluffs of the river
—LEWIS, JULY 23, 1806

CAMP DISAPPOINTMENT ON (CUT BANK CREEK)   JULY 22 TO 25, 1806

CAMP DISAPPOINTMENT CAMPSITE   JULY 22 TO 25, 1806

I thought it unnecessary to proceed
further ... the rocky mountains to the
S.W ... are partially covered with snow
—LEWIS, JULY 22, 1806

Overcast skies prevented Lewis from establishing his location from celestial readings so he called it "Camp Disappointment." On the morning of July 26th they headed south to pick up the south fork of Maria's River (Two Medicine River). They had seen evidence of Indians, but had seen none.

BLUFFS SOUTHSIDE OF THE RIVER   JULY 26, 1806

THE SOUTH FORK OF MARIA'S RIVER (TWO MEDICINE RIVER)   JULY 26, 1806

*I discovered to my left at the distance of a
mile an assembleage of about 30 horses.*
—LEWIS, JULY 26, 1806

Drouillard was riding along the river, looking for deer, while Lewis and the Field brothers traveled along the bluffs south of the river.

Lewis observed eight Blackfeet Indians through his spyglass. They were all watching Drouillard making his way along the river. Lewis slowly approached the Indians. The Indians were startled when they finally saw the white men. After a tense initial standoff, the two parties were soon shaking hands and smoking.

That evening they all camped together by the river. The Indians were upset when Lewis conveyed that the Americans would soon be trading with all Indians in the west, including their enemies.

Just before sunrise, the Blackfeet stole all the guns and in their attempted escape Reubin Field killed one of the fleeing Indians with his knife. A scuffle ensued but the guns were recovered.

CAMP AND FIGHT SITE   JULY 27, 1806

The Indians attempted to run off the horses as they fled. Lewis pursued the Indians while Drouillard and the Field brothers rounded up as many horses as they could. When one of the Indians pulled out his gun Lewis shot him in the belly. As the Indian fell, mortally wounded, he fired a shot past Lewis' head.

Although the six remaining Indians escaped with most of the horses, Lewis and his men still had enough horses for their escape to the Missouri.

ESCAPE ROUTE, SOUTHEAST OF THE FIGHT SITE   JULY 27, 1806

*my indian horse carried me very well in short
much better than my own*

—LEWIS, JULY 27, 1806

Lewis and his men escaped through the open country, south-east of the fight site. Fearing the Blackfeet would regroup and be in pursuit, Lewis and his men rode all day and most of the night. They traveled all the way to the Missouri by the next morning.

Lewis' crew met the remainder of his party and Clark's portage crew near the mouth of Maria's River and they continued down the Missouri to the Yellowstone. Clark had arrived ahead of Lewis and left him a note saying that the mosquitoes were so bad that he had to move on down the river.

On August 12th Lewis caught up with Clark, and the Corps of Discovery was together again. Two days later they were back at the Mandan villages.

Traveling with the current, the explorers made good time on the final leg of the journey. A shout of joy came from the men when they saw their first cow—a true sign of civilization.

On September 23rd the Corps of Discovery arrived in St. Louis to a huge throng of celebrating citizens. President Jefferson was ecstatic—the goals of the expedition had been fulfilled. Captains Lewis and Clark were heroes and were rightly rewarded for their accomplishment. Their adventure accelerated the exploration and white settlement of the western frontier. Many expedition members returned to the lands they had traversed to further explore and develop. The lives and ways of the native inhabitants would be changed forever. Some adapted—many did not.

The Lewis and Clark Expedition had accomplished the improbable—the odds had been against them. Rushing, frigid snow-melt waters constantly surged against the unbelievably strong men as they forged their way upstream. Grizzly bears made life exciting and mosquitoes made life miserable. Hail, torrents of rain, the flesh-freezing cold of the Mandan village, and the oppressive heat of the high plains were challenged and conquered. The constant threat of annihilation from less-than-friendly natives was always with them, yet without the native peoples' assistance and benevolence the mission most likely would have failed.

MISSOURI RIVER, UP RIVER FROM MARIA'S RIVER   JULY 28, 1806

unspeakable satisfaction to see our canoes coming down ... imbarking without loss of time
—LEWIS, JULY 28, 1806